AWESOME AMBULANCES

Tony Mitton and
Ant Parker

KINGFISHER

If you've had an accident,
or if you're very sick,
an ambulance assists you.
Its response is very quick.

When the station takes a call
to say that you're in need,
an ambulance will get to you
by driving at great speed.

To clear the road ahead of it,
its siren fills the air.
It tells the other drivers
someone's hurt or needing care.

For extra visibility,
especially at night,
an ambulance's beacons
will flash their vivid lights.

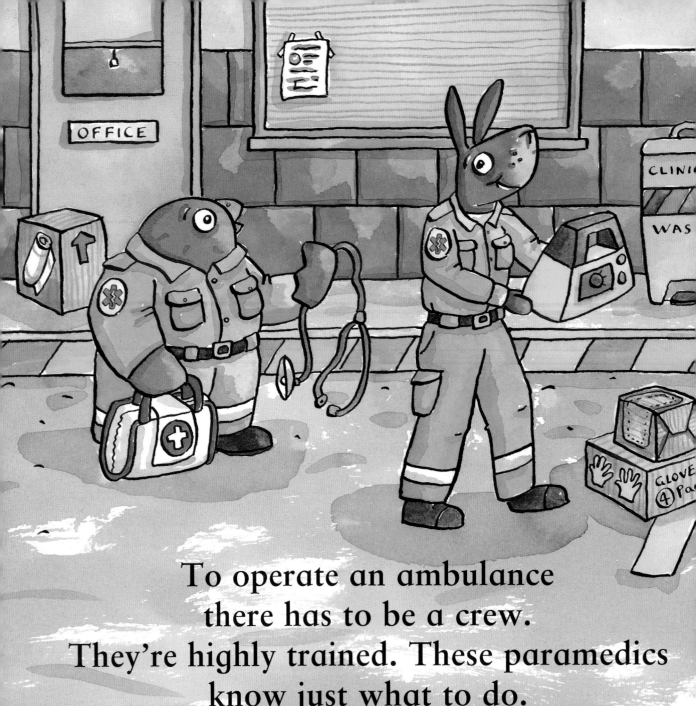

To operate an ambulance
there has to be a crew.
They're highly trained. These paramedics
know just what to do.

They carry the equipment
for every situation.
They check to see it's all on board
while waiting at the station.

They store all kinds of bandages,
in case you start to bleed.

To deal with pain and problems,
they've medicine you might need.

There's oxygen to help you breathe,
if you're really sick.

And if you have a broken bone
these splints should do the trick.

For people who are very weak
and cannot move or stand,
the paramedics use a bed on wheels
to lend a hand.

This bed is called a stretcher.
It gives a gentle ride.
And after that it's folded up
and packed away inside.

When the patient's safely in
the ambulance at last
it's time to get them treated
at the hospital – and fast!

The driver travels speedily,
but keeps the vehicle steady.
The hospital is radioed
to have them at the ready.

On the way the paramedics
use their skill and care
to keep the patient comfortable
until arriving there.

Hooray for Awesome Ambulances
ready round the clock!

Ambulance bits

First-aid kit
this carries equipment for many emergency situations

Collapsible stretcher
this is used to move patients who are too hurt or sick to walk

Oxygen tan
this carries the oxyge for the oxygen mask

Disposable gloves
these keep the paramedics' hands free from germs and infection

Splint
this will keep a broken arm or leg straight until it can be treated

Oxygen mas
this gives oxygen to patients when they're not breathing properly

Plasters
these patch up very small cuts or wounds

Bandages
these are used to cover wounds

Oxymeter
this measures how much oxygen is in a person's blood